D09929801

Seth MacFarlane
and Family Guy

Seth MacFarlane and Family Guy

Gail Snyder

ReferencePoint
Press®

San Diego, CA

38212006487943
Main Young Adlt Biography
M143ss
Snyder, Gail
Seth MacFarlane and Family guy

© 2016 ReferencePoint Press, Inc.
Printed in the United States

For more information, contact:
ReferencePoint Press, Inc.
PO Box 27779
San Diego, CA 92198
www.ReferencePointPress.com

LIBRARY OF CONGRESS CATALOGING-IN-PUBLICATION DATA

Snyder, Gail.
   Seth MacFarlane and Family guy / by Gail Snyder.
       pages cm. -- (Contemporary cartoon creators)
   ISBN-13: 978-1-60152-864-3 (hardback)
   ISBN-10: 1-60152-864-7 (hardback)
   1. MacFarlane, Seth, 1973---Juvenile literature. 2. Animators--United States--Biography--Juvenile literature. I. Title.
   NC1766.U52M3825 2015
   741.58092--dc23
   [B]

                                                                           2015000379

CONTENTS

Humor on the Edge

The 1993 film *Philadelphia* tells the tragic story of a young lawyer who learns he has contracted acquired immune deficiency syndrome (AIDS). As the lawyer battles AIDS, he also battles against the prejudice of the senior partners of his law firm, who have little empathy for his plight and no wish to help him. Both the film itself as well as its star, Tom Hanks, won universal acclaim for telling a story of social injustice while calling attention to the horrific effects of the disease on ordinary people.

But when Peter Griffin saw the film, he laughed out loud. The numbskull star of the animated TV show *Family Guy* actually thought he was watching a comedy. In the 1999 premiere episode, Griffin is sitting in a movie theater when he notices Hanks on-screen. It seems Hanks has starred in one of Griffin's favorite films—the comedy *Big*, the story of a young boy who wakes up one morning to discover he has turned into an adult. Since the dim-witted Griffin thinks Hanks stars in comedies only, when he sees Hanks on-screen in *Philadelphia* he gets ready to laugh.

"Tom Hanks, that's it," Griffin says. "Aw, funny guy, Tom Hanks. Everything he says is a stitch."[1] When the Hanks character announces he has contracted AIDS, Griffin bursts into a gale of laughter.

The notion that laughs can be found in the dramatic story of a dying AIDS patient may seem repugnant to some, but not to Seth MacFarlane. The creator of *Family Guy*—and the voice of Peter Griffin—has established himself in Hollywood as an animation pro-

> "It got a huge laugh at the senior screening. It wasn't a conscious decision to shock; I just thought it was funny."[2]
>
> —*Family Guy* creator Seth MacFarlane.

ducer who encounters few barriers when it comes to making people laugh. If it happens in society—whether it is AIDS affliction, racial stereotyping, or prejudice against the physically disabled—MacFarlane believes there are gags to be mined.

The episode in which Griffin guffaws at an AIDS-stricken character was actually conceived by MacFarlane years before he began producing *Family Guy*. As a senior in college, he produced an animated film with a similar scene. "It got a huge laugh at the senior screening," says MacFarlane. "It wasn't a conscious decision to shock; I just thought it was funny."[2]

Seth MacFarlane poses in front of an image of the Griffin family from his show, Family Guy. MacFarlane's edgy humor has earned him legions of fans and made Family Guy a respected—if controversial—animated adult series.

Inspired by Groening

Certainly, MacFarlane is not the first producer to employ animation as a medium for finding comedy in serious social issues. MacFarlane acknowledges his debt to the longtime hit TV show *The Simpsons*, created and produced by Matt Groening, which finds a lot of humor in social issues in addition to the slapstick foibles of the Simpson family. But in *Family Guy*, MacFarlane has taken the comedic threshold established by Groening and ratcheted it up a notch. "[The AIDS] joke is certainly not a joke you would see on *The Simpsons*," says MacFarlane. "That show had taken edginess in prime-time animation to a certain level. I was trying to take it to the next level. The AIDS joke is one instance."[3]

MacFarlane credits Groening with inspiring him to abandon his original plan of working for the Walt Disney animation studio in favor of making edgier cartoons for older audiences who find humor in what is often a darker side of life. For his part, Groening says he sees a lot of himself in MacFarlane: the desire to push the edges of comedy and poke fun at institutions in American life that people do not often regard with a sense of humor. Says Groening, "I have more in common with Seth than anybody I work with. . . . If you can make the person who disagrees with the joke laugh, then it's good. If it's just preaching to the choir, then I don't like it as much."[4]

> "I have more in common with Seth than anybody I work with."[4]
>
> —Matt Groening, creator of *The Simpsons*.

Groening acknowledges that one of his sons is a dedicated fan of *Family Guy*. Groening's son is not alone. In fact, according to the trade publication *Inside TV*, *Family Guy* was the twenty-fourth-highest-rated broadcast TV show in the 2013–2014 season, whereas *The Simpsons* finished in thirty-sixth place. Moreover, another MacFarlane-produced animated show, *American Dad!*—a spoof about a spy trying to maintain a suburban lifestyle—was close behind in forty-second place.

Crossover Appeal

On September 28, 2014, fans of *Family Guy* and *The Simpsons* were offered a rare treat: A crossover episode in which characters from the two shows appeared together on-screen. (Officially, the show appeared in the TV listings as an episode of *Family Guy*.) During the show, the characters poked fun at feminism, sexist attitudes, and violence on television. There was even a gag made about sexual assault.

Such jokes may be taboo on some TV shows, but MacFarlane's fans demand that style of humor in his work. When the crossover episode aired, it drew some 8.5 million viewers—about the size of the audiences of the two shows combined. This meant that *Family Guy* fans received a dose of what they have come to expect from MacFarlane's work, and *Simpsons* fans may have received a peek at an even edgier style of humor than they have been accustomed to seeing.

CHAPTER ONE

Born to Cartoon

Home to fewer than three thousand people, Kent, Connecticut, is made up of a series of hamlets with picturesque names such as Bulls Bridge, Flanders, Kent Hollow, and the Cobble. Visitors will find farms and scenic waterfalls on the Housatonic River, as well as portions of the Appalachian Trail. In this most idyllic example of small-town America, TV's edgiest animator was born and raised.

Seth Woodbury MacFarlane was born October 26, 1973, the son of Ron and Perry MacFarlane, both of whom came of age during the 1960s: a time when the youth counterculture movement was fueled by protests against the Vietnam War and by rebellion against the older generation's ideas about clothing, hair length, drug use, and sexuality.

> "There's a side of him that I can't quite get to. He never really liked being hugged or touched."[6]
>
> —Ron MacFarlane, Seth's father.

The couple met in a health food store in which Perry was shopping and Ron was playing guitar. Ron, who wore long sideburns, attended the 1969 Woodstock Music and Art Fair, the landmark three-day rock concert in Bethel, New York, in which a half million young people gathered together to celebrate their culture, listen to performances by the hottest rock stars of the era, and most significantly, demand an end to the Vietnam War.

According to MacFarlane, his parents were the type of people who were willing to accept whatever career path their children chose. "They were ex-hippies," MacFarlane says of his parents, "so they weren't forcing me to be a doctor or an accountant or anything like that."[5]

The Middle-Class MacFarlanes

At first Ron and Perry pursued the counterculture life in Kent—their first home was a log cabin they built in the woods. Yet by the time

Seth and his sister, Rachael, were born, Ron and Perry were becoming more like mainstream middle-class citizens.

Perry found a job as a school administrator, and Ron worked first as a butcher and then as a music history teacher. They worked hard to foster their children's artistic sensibilities—Seth as an artist and Rachael as a singer—and were laid-back enough to allow the entire family to eat dinner while they watched television programs together.

A quiet, serious boy who wore glasses, MacFarlane fell in love with cartoons almost immediately. As a toddler he was already making easily recognizable drawings of Fred Flintstone and Woody Woodpecker. The drawings, often made on paper grocery bags from the store at which his father worked, were so good that his parents, family friends, and neighbors saved them.

But there was little doubt that MacFarlane was the type of boy who would disappear into his own world. "There's a side of him that I can't quite get to," Ron MacFarlane says. "He never really liked being hugged or touched."[6]

First produced by Walter Lantz Productions in the 1940s, the classic cartoon character Woody Woodpecker remained a staple of children's television for many decades. Seth MacFarlane was able to draw Woody Woodpecker and other television cartoon characters at a very early age.

Yet despite MacFarlane's reserve, he led a happy childhood in which his parents tried to change one thing only about him: his peculiar way of holding a drawing pencil so that it was completely vertical. They could not convince him to slant the instrument the way most people do. So they gave up trying.

First Cartoon

MacFarlane produced his first animated cartoon when he was four. Drawn on long slips of paper that could be unspooled to create the illusion of movement, the cartoon told a humorous yet true story about two dogs and their encounter with an automatic dog biscuit dispenser. The story had been shared with MacFarlane by his babysitter. Even at the age of four, MacFarlane recognized its comic potential. In the cartoon, one dog quickly learned that pressing a pedal released the dog treats. The second dog was unable to figure out how the dispenser worked. Instead, he knocked the dispenser over, sending treats everywhere. The babysitter was amazed at how well MacFarlane brought the story to life.

By the time MacFarlane created his first cartoon, he was like most children his age—a big fan of cartoons. But unlike other children, who are content with simply watching animated entertainment, the young MacFarlane was attracted more by the creative process of cartooning. Says *New York Times* entertainment critic Bruce Newman:

> "One of the things Seth MacFarlane liked about animation when he was growing up was the way it elasticized reality. Anvils dropped without consequences and skunks sang in French."[7]
>
> —Bruce Newman, *New York Times* entertainment critic.

One of the things Seth MacFarlane liked about animation when he was growing up was the way it elasticized reality. Anvils dropped without consequences and skunks sang in French . . . he could retreat from a world where people treated him, shockingly, like a child and enter one where he was in complete control. There, in the manner of a visiting deity, he spoke for everyone, he had all the money in the world, and a thought never entered anyone's head that he didn't put there.[7]

A Celebrity at Eleven

In 1985 Dorothy Lane, a reporter from the *Litchfield County Times*, visited Seth MacFarlane's home to interview the eleven-year-old about his life as a working cartoonist, a life he was allowed to pursue only after dinner and homework were finished. At the time of the reporter's visit, MacFarlane was working on a cartoon story called "Walter Crouton Moves to Kent," which he hoped would attract the interest of a book publisher. The story was an extension of a newspaper comic strip he drew for a rival newspaper, the *Kent Good Times Dispatch.* As the reporter looked on, MacFarlane drew one of his characters, Walter Crouton's wife, Lady Bubble Button. Lane wrote about MacFarlane:

> He has not had any formal art lessons, but his years of experience show when he takes his Bic Roller pen in hand to demonstrate. Lady Bubble Button Crouton appears in one continuous, sure line, beginning with a profile, then mouth and eyes and long curly hair. Her dress, then arms and legs and high-heeled shoes complete the character in typical costume. The young artist says he wants to become a professional cartoonist, to write and draw comic books, do TV specials, and, his latest passion, animation.

> Although he clearly anticipated the direction he was headed, MacFarlane expressed some reservations about animating television cartoons. He said he found printed comic strips funnier than animated cartoons. "TV leaves the adventure in, with lots of characters getting beat up, but it takes the humor out," he said.

Dorothy Lane, "Kent Student Is a Working Cartoonist," *Litchfield County Times*, January 18, 1985, p. 29.

Voice Impressionist

Even as he worked on early drawing and animation projects, MacFarlane and his sister began entertaining their parents with homemade puppets and voice impressions. Rachael recalls, "My father has videos of us making paper-bag puppets and subjecting our parents to awful hourlong shows where we'd do the voices. [Seth's] puppets were incredible."[8]

Meanwhile, by the time MacFarlane was ready to attend Kent's only public elementary school, the Kent Center School, he was already singing and developing his stage presence by participating in community theater musicals. His evolving musical tastes made for some strained moments in the family car, at least as far as his sister was concerned. Rachael recalls, "When we were kids and we'd be driving in the car, he'd want to listen to movie scores. . . . I wanted Tiffany or Debbie Gibson, and he wanted the soundtrack to *Back to the Future*."[9]

By middle school age in the mid-1980s, he was ready to take his voice impressions more public by trying them out on his sister's friends. Says Rachael, who is two years younger than Seth:

> I remember having a dance party in the backyard when I was 11 or 12, and Seth wanted to DJ. He was great. And then, all of a sudden, the music stops and he's imitating [President] Ronald Reagan doing an interview with [presidential candidate] Michael Dukakis. He's bouncing between the two voices, and my friends are like, "What is this?" But that was Seth's deal. And everyone just sort of accepted him. He was not a typical child at all; there was something special about him.[10]

Bruce Adams was MacFarlane's social studies teacher at Kent Center, which he attended from kindergarten through eighth grade. Adams recalls MacFarlane as a boy mature for his age and clearly headed for a bigger future than could be found in his tiny hometown. "He was hilarious, even when he was in seventh and eighth grades,"[11] Adams says. One day MacFarlane made a quick sketch of Adams confronting a school bully. Adams liked the drawing so much that he has kept it for more than thirty years.

While attending Kent Center, MacFarlane was also well known for his messy school locker—filled not only with his books, coat, and gloves, but also his many sketches. His friend Paulette Menniti-Pizzo says, "If Seth went to his locker, everyone stepped aside because when he opened it his whole world came falling out. He had that kind of amazing mind."[12]

First Controversy

The students at Kent Center were not the only people in town to have gained an insight into how MacFarlane's mind works. When MacFarlane was nine years old, he began drawing his own weekly newspaper cartoon. Titled *Walter Crouton* (the title was based on the name of television news anchor Walter Cronkite), the cartoon appeared in the *Kent Good Times Dispatch*, which paid him about ten dollars a cartoon.

Some of MacFarlane's newspaper cartoons were purely whimsical. For example, one cartoon had some fun with reversing the roles of animals and people. In the drawing, two mice dressed as humans sit at their kitchen table. Visible in the distant background, near the floorboard, is a tiny suburban tract house with a car parked in front. The cartoon's punchline features one mouse saying to the other, "Uh-oh, Harold, we have humans."

> "If Seth went to his locker, everyone stepped aside because when he opened it his whole world came falling out. He had that kind of amazing mind."[12]
>
> —Paulette Menniti-Pizzo, Seth MacFarlane's childhood friend.

But MacFarlane soon grew bolder; it did not take long before he incurred the displeasure of the local priest for a cartoon he drew about the Catholic sacrament of communion in which the priest symbolically turns wine and a sacramental wafer into the flesh and blood of Jesus Christ. The *Walter Crouton* strip that drew an angry letter from the priest featured a man receiving communion and asking the priest if he can also have an order of fries. Although MacFarlane had perhaps innocently created controversy in his town, the paper did not censor him and continued running his comic strip until he left home to attend college.

Mischievous Mother

According to MacFarlane, the style of humor he displayed in the *Walter Crouton* cartoon stems from his mother's side of the family. Members of her family, he says, harbored an appreciation for salty language, potty humor, and all manner of edgy comedy. MacFarlane says, "The style of humor that you'll see in [*Family Guy*] is the same kind of tasteless humor that you'd find around my house when I was growing up. Some of the foulest jokes that I ever heard came from my mother."[13]

That humor apparently started at MacFarlane's birth when he was given the middle name of Woodbury, a name he shared with many male members of his mother's family. The original Woodbury was a gruff, colorful ne'er-do-well who lived during the turn of the twentieth century in Seth's great-grandmother's hometown in Maine. She described him as the funniest person she ever met. "Most of the jokes we make in our house, we would just never even dream of making anywhere else," says MacFarlane. "Just sick, horrible stuff."[14]

Perry MacFarlane also possessed a mischievous nature. Seth recalls that when his mother was in high school, she teased one of her fellow students, a boy who had polio, a viral disease that often leads to muscle weakness. When the boy was not looking, Perry removed the rubber shock absorbers from the bottom of his crutches. Some people might say that what Perry did was mean, but Seth disagrees. "Isn't that treating the handicapped just like other people? I bet that kid never felt like he fit in more than he did that day,"[15] he says.

High School Years

As MacFarlane employed his style of humor in the *Walter Crouton* comic strip, he found himself regaining an interest in the form of comic art that he first discovered as a four-year-old: animation. As he grew into his teenage years, MacFarlane discovered the Nickelodeon program *Standby: Lights! Camera! Action!* Hosted by actor Leonard Nimoy, the show, which ran from 1982 to 1984, delved into all aspects of filmmaking. One episode in particular stood out to MacFarlane: It featured a college student who made an animated film. Watching the episode, MacFarlane believed that he too could make an animated film. He convinced his parents to buy him a used 8-millimeter movie camera, which he used to create *Space Pirates*, his first animated film. It was produced for a school assignment, and MacFarlane concedes the animation was amateurish—but it was a start. "I really didn't know what I was doing," he says. "I was shooting every movement on 12 frames when I should have been shooting it on 1 or 2. As a result, it moved very, very slowly."[16]

Leonard Nimoy, best-known as Dr. Spock in the Star Trek television series and movies, hosted a TV show that inspired a young Seth MacFarlane. That show, which ran on Nickelodeon in the 1980s, delved into all aspects of filmmaking, including the making of an animated film.

MacFarlane spent his high school years at Kent School, a private college preparatory academy he was able to attend for free because his mother worked there as an administrator. Most of the school's students lived on campus, but MacFarlane continued to live at home.

He found himself at odds with his wealthier peers, who had grown up in conservative homes and whose parents were hardly the type to have been at Woodstock. Already politically liberal like his parents, he often found himself in debates against supporters of then president George H.W. Bush. While at Kent he continued his musical tradition, playing trombone in band and appearing in school musicals such as *Anything Goes*, *Little Shop of Horrors*, and *Carousel*.

Although he was capable and smart, he did not always try his best in class, sometimes earning grades of C minus in science despite being a self-confessed nerd. He threw himself into subjects that interested him; in school, that meant art class, where he earned his school's top prize at graduation in 1991. At home, MacFarlane turned into a huge fan of the TV series *Star Trek*. He liked the program so much that he created a detailed version of the *Starship Enterprise*'s bridge out of cardboard; his parents allowed it to take up a room in their house.

MacFarlane Goes to College

When it came time to apply to college, MacFarlane knew exactly what he wanted to declare as his major. Certain that he wanted to be an animator, he applied to several art schools, including a university in Florida that offered students the opportunity to intern at the Walt Disney Studio. At his mother's suggestion he also applied to the Rhode Island School of Design (RISD) in Providence, Rhode Island. He elected to attend RISD in 1991—immediately after finishing high school—because it was closer to home. He credits his professors there with encouraging him to develop his own animation style—one that was more in tune with *The Simpsons* than with the Disney-style entertainment that originally drew his interest.

Extremely casual about his personal appearance, MacFarlane stood out on campus as the one undergraduate whose clothes did not make an artistic statement: He wore the same bland rugby shirt to all his classes. Outside of class he gained a reputation as a stand-up comic who performed voice impressions at local comedy clubs. He struck comic gold with an impression in which he mimicked President Bill Clinton talking with the animated dog Scooby-Doo. As a student at

RISD, MacFarlane came to realize that he wanted to specialize in animation that would make people laugh.

The Life of Larry

As things turned out, MacFarlane's senior animation project made a lot of people laugh. As a senior at RISD, he was required to produce a thesis film, and while his fellow students showed their professors storyboards of films that aimed for artistic quality, MacFarlane's storyboard aimed more for comic content. Says MacFarlane, "I just wanted to make people laugh and I remember taking a lot of guff from my professors about that. I showed my storyboard to my film professor, and she said, 'I'm really worried that you're wasting your time on what is essentially a lot of bathroom humor.'"[17]

MacFarlane titled his ten-minute thesis film *The Life of Larry*. In it he appeared on camera to announce his idea for an animated cartoon series and to briefly introduce the characters that would populate it: Larry Cummings, a loveable but bumbling New England father who longed to be closer to his offspring; Milt, his overweight son; Lois, his wife; and Steve, their cynical talking dog. As part of their normal daily routine, Larry and Steve watch *Star Trek*, allowing MacFarlane to poke fun at the iconic characters from that show that he knew so well. The short feature contained many of the ingredients—and jokes— that eventually found their way into the first episode of *Family Guy*. "If I thought of a gag that was too hilarious not to do, I would try to force it into the script. It was this meandering train-of-thought sort of thing. But it got a lot of laughs,"[18] MacFarlane says.

MacFarlane's final cut of *The Life of Larry* was well received by fellow students, who convinced MacFarlane that he had made a good film by laughing in all the right places. Two of his professors entered the film in an animation contest sponsored by Hanna-Barbera; one of the oldest and biggest animation studios, it was responsible for iconic television cartoons such as *The Flintstones*, *Yogi Bear*, and *The Jetsons*. Steve Subotnick, one of the professors who thought MacFarlane belonged at Hanna-Barbera, had this to say about *The Life of Larry*: "It was done really well and it was hilarious, but as you can see from what he's produced, it is humor that thrives on being right at the edge of what is tolerable."[19] Though its humor was cruder than what filled the more family-friendly Hanna-Barbera classics, *The Life of Larry* won the contest.

Working on *Johnny Bravo*

MacFarlane's film and his award for winning the Hanna-Barbera contest helped convince executives at Hanna-Barbera that he should be working at the studio. Weeks before his 1996 graduation, MacFarlane was offered a writing and animation job at Hanna-Barbera. That meant that at twenty-one, MacFarlane was finally off to Hollywood to live out the first chapter of the dream he had begun formulating as a four-year-old. His initial salary was not much, and MacFarlane had to live in a tiny one-bedroom apartment with no air-conditioning—a required comfort to most people who endure the year-round heat of Southern California. Nevertheless, MacFarlane was now getting paid for doing work he loved.

At Hanna-Barbera, MacFarlane was assigned to work on two of the studio's new cartoons, *Johnny Bravo* and *Cow and Chicken*. The creator of *Johnny Bravo* is Van Partible, who, like MacFarlane, conceived the character of Johnny Bravo for his senior animation thesis project at Loyola Marymount University in Los Angeles. Partible based the main character on a vain bodybuilder whom he believed sounded a lot like singer Elvis Presley. The show's running gag finds Bravo believing he is a lady's man. But women uniformly reject him. Moreover, in every episode Johnny fails to get the message. MacFarlane served as an animator for the show and also wrote several of the scripts, which were appropriate for children but sometimes contained a few jokes that were more likely appreciated by adult viewers.

Johnny Bravo became a cult hit for the up-and-coming Cartoon Network. The show provided MacFarlane with the training he needed to eventually write his own television shows. Indeed, one MacFarlane-authored episode featured Adam West, the actor who played Batman on the 1960s television show about the comic book hero and whom MacFarlane would cast in the role of mayor on *Family Guy*.

Best known for his portrayal of Batman in the campy 1960s television series about the Caped Crusader, actor Adam West is a regular on the convention circuit. Here, at a collectors show in 2011, he signs photos of characters he has played, including Family Guy*'s Mayor West.*

Larry Returns

In addition to his work on *Johnny Bravo*, MacFarlane also worked as a writer on Hanna-Barbera's *Cow and Chicken* series, another Cartoon Network program airing in 1997. The series and its gags were based on the premise that siblings and their parents could be of different

Angering His Former Headmaster

Prior to the premiere of *Family Guy*, Seth MacFarlane heard some criticism about the series from a most unexpected source: the headmaster of Kent School, the school MacFarlane attended in the late 1980s and early 1990s.

Richardson Schell, an Episcopal priest, was unhappy when he learned—just days before the series premiered—that *Family Guy* featured a loutish family with the same last name as his assistant, Elaine Griffin. When MacFarlane refused his request to change the family's last name—an impossibility since the show was too far into production—Schell organized a campaign that called on sponsors to boycott the show, the humor of which he found crude and offensive. He formed his own group, Proud Sponsors USA, writing letters to ask advertisers to pull their ads from the program. The boycott was ineffective, but MacFarlane's mother, who was still working at Kent School, quit her job in support of her son.

In defending the program, Fox vice president for corporate communications Jeff De Rome said, "This is a satire of political correctness. An argument could be made that an irreverent comedy that can't raise a clergyman's eyebrows isn't doing its job."

Quoted in Lawrie Mifflin, "Irate Headmaster, Irreverent Alumnus: The *Family Guy* Saga," *New York Times,* July 1, 1999, p. E1.

species. Cow is a seven-year-old female and Chicken is her eleven-year-old brother. Their parents are humans whose torsos and faces are never seen.

In his free time while working at Hanna-Barbera, MacFarlane re-shot *The Life of Larry* into a new animated short feature, titled *Larry & Steve*. Once again, the feature revolved around a talking dog and his dim-witted owner. This time the dog, speaking in MacFarlane's natural voice, served as the narrator, explaining the comic events that had befallen him since the incompetent Larry adopted him from the animal shelter. In 1997 the Cartoon Network aired *Larry & Steve* on its series *What a Cartoon!*, which featured independently produced short animations.

With an eye toward helping Hanna-Barbera return to prime-time animation, the company's head of development introduced MacFarlane to executives from the Fox Broadcasting Company. After watching the *Larry & Steve* short feature, they invited him to produce a pilot for their network, providing him with a $50,000 advance. Although that may sound like a lot of money, it represents only about one-twentieth of what a pilot usually costs to produce. MacFarlane seized the opportunity and began drawing the first sketches for what would become *Family Guy*.

CHAPTER TWO

Family Guy: TV's Most Shocking Show

Seth MacFarlane spent months drawing images for the pilot at his kitchen table, finally producing an eight-minute version of *Family Guy* for network broadcast. After seeing the brief pilot, Fox executives green-lighted the series. Says Sandy Grushow, president of 20th Century Fox Television, "That the network ordered a series off of eight minutes of film is just testimony to how powerful those eight minutes were. There are very few people in their early 20's who have ever created a television series."[20]

Family Guy made its debut on network television on January 31, 1999—right after Fox's telecast of the Super Bowl. The show imported the *Life of Larry* and *Larry & Steve* dynamic of a bumbling dog owner and his pet (renamed Peter Griffin and Brian, respectively) and expanded the supporting family to include wife, Lois; older sister, Meg; middle child, Chris; and baby, Stewie. The audience for the *Family Guy* debut was recorded at 22 million. Given the size of the audience, Fox believed MacFarlane had produced a hit and offered him $1 million a year to continue production. "Sit down when I tell you this," he told his mother in a phone call. "They are paying me a million dollars a year."[21]

For a young animator still in his mid-twenties, the salary seemed astronomical. But MacFarlane earned his money. Fox gave MacFarlane a small budget, meaning he lacked the team of animators and technicians assigned to produce *The Simpsons*. Therefore, he found himself doing much of the hands-on animation himself—while also carrying out the other jobs of producer and voice actor. Like *The Simpsons*, MacFarlane centers the show on a family, the Griffins, as they navigate life in fictional Quahog, Rhode Island. Along the way, Peter's moronic and impulsive behaviors, Brian's intellectual wit, and Stewie's lust for power become lenses through which MacFarlane provides both insight into and satire of contemporary culture. The humor is often crude, and nothing—from politics to popular television—is spared playful and pointed mockery.

Controversy and Cancellation

As the show found more viewers, Fox increased the budget. But as the show gained in popularity, so did the backlash against MacFarlane's brand of humor, which operates on the supposition that nothing is sacred. For example, during one *Family Guy* episode Jesus Christ shows up at the local mall, where he encounters the Griffins. Jesus admits he will not be spending his birthday with his indifferent father and confesses that he has never had a date. The portrayal of Christ angered many Christians, but the show consistently ruffled feathers while maintaining a large audience share early on. The Parents Television Council criticized the show for its emphasis on gags dependent on sexual themes. Other viewers remarked that the show wallowed in its crudity. Ken Tucker, TV critic for the magazine *Entertainment Weekly*, said the show's content lacked originality. He commented, "[*Family Guy* is] conceived by a singularly sophomoric mind that lacks any reference point beyond other TV shows."[22]

Moreover, despite *Family Guy*'s initial success, by the third season the ratings started dropping. This was due in part to the network's decision to move the show around in its schedule, ultimately placing it in competition with the popular situation comedy *Friends*. In 2002 *Family Guy* was canceled.

> "That the network ordered a series off of eight minutes of film [of *Family Guy*] is just testimony to how powerful those eight minutes were. There are very few people in their early 20's who have ever created a television series."[20]
>
> —Sandy Grushow, president of 20th Century Fox Television.

The Griffins Return to Prime Time

MacFarlane literally went back to the drawing table, working on concepts for new shows to pitch to network bosses. Meanwhile, reruns of *Family Guy* started airing nightly as part of the Cartoon Network's

A still of the Griffin family at a picnic. From left to right: Brian, the dog; Meg; Chris; Peter; Lois; and Stewie. Although Family Guy *often critiques popular social issues, using a nuclear family as a focal point allows MacFarlane and his writers to explore and poke fun at family relationships as well.*

evening package of shows known as Adult Swim. The show quickly became the most popular feature on Adult Swim. Moreover, in 2003 Fox packaged a season of *Family Guy* episodes in a DVD boxed set. It sold 3 million copies. By then the Fox executives decided they had erred in canceling *Family Guy* and invited MacFarlane back with a budget big enough for him to hire a large staff.

No one was more surprised than MacFarlane about the show's unlikely comeback. Called to a meeting with Gary Newman, 20th Century Fox Television's president, he did not know what to expect. MacFarlane recalled, "[Newman] said, 'We'd like to put this back into production,' and I almost fell out of my chair."[23] The revived show's premiere aired in May 2005, drawing 12 million viewers.

Now just thirty-two years old, MacFarlane had gone from drawing comic strips for a small-town newspaper to being one of the hottest animation producers in Hollywood. He achieved his success through his natural talent as an artist and impressionist, hard work, and a keen insight into what makes people laugh.

MacFarlane's Ongoing Role in *Family Guy*

Once MacFarlane had a large staff at his disposal, the artistic process changed. For example, he no longer draws all the stills by hand or writes every word of dialogue. Today it takes a staff of more than three hundred people on two continents to produce *Family Guy*. Working in studios and offices in Los Angeles, writers conceive the gags that pour out of the mouths of the characters, and actors lend their voices to those characters. In the studio where the actors record their lines, technicians control the quality of the audio, and a director decides whether the acting meets the standards expected by the audience. It is not unusual for the actors to run through the dialogue several times.

Meanwhile, artists work with ink and paper as well as digital tools on computer screens, creating images. The drawings that leave the Los Angeles studio are not much more than rough outlines of each episode. The images head next for a studio in South Korea, where the final full-color episodes are animated and made ready for broadcast.

Watching over virtually every facet of the show's production is MacFarlane. He is part of the writing team. He provides the voices for nearly a dozen regular and cameo characters. He still provides art for the show—producing rough sketches for some of the key scenes—before they are turned over to the show's animators. "I still do a lot of the drawing on a daily basis,"[24] he says.

A snapshot of the energy that goes into each *Family Guy* episode can be found at the table read, the first opportunity for the actors to speak their lines. Sitting around a table, scripts in hand, the actors perform a read-through of the episode. During the table read, jokes are tested, the timing of the dialogue is worked out, and the actors experiment with the nuances of their voices, giving human qualities to the characters.

Man of Many Voices

Since MacFarlane provides the voices for so many characters, he spends a lot of time during the table read making sure the sounds uttered by Peter and the others are exactly how he wants the audience to hear them. (In addition to Peter, MacFarlane also voices the Griffin baby, Stewie; talking dog, Brian; and Quagmire, Peter's morally bankrupt friend, among others.)

During the table read for a 2012 episode, titled "Friends Without Benefits," MacFarlane demonstrated how he gives voice to Peter: He opened his mouth wide and made the sounds of Peter's voice re-

Seth MacFarlane reads for an episode of Family Guy. *MacFarlane has a close attachment to his show, actively helping with scripts and voicing several characters including Peter and Stewie Griffin and their dog, Brian.*

verberate off a cheek. "My daughter is going on a date," MacFarlane lamented in Peter's typical tone of sarcasm. "Is there a slow-down button on this life-thing?"[25] When the other actors around the table broke into laughter, MacFarlane knew he had caught Peter's tone of voice exactly.

Next, he demonstrated how he gives voice to Stewie, the Griffins' superintelligent baby notable for his football-shaped head and his designs on world domination. (Stewie's character is inspired by MacFarlane's cousin Tyler. As a four-year-old—and within MacFarlane's earshot—Tyler once responded to his aunt's suggestion that she would see him later by saying he would see her in hell.) To speak as Stewie, MacFarlane took pains to tighten the muscles in his face, jut out his chin, then utter the character's dialogue—seemingly through his nose. Performing Brian's lines requires no special effort, since the wisecracking dog shares MacFarlane's normal speaking voice. Nevertheless, voicing Brian's lines—and those of many other characters—can give MacFarlane a recurring sore throat.

When the table read ended, some of the actors chatted among themselves or with members of the writing staff to assess their performances. MacFarlane did not dawdle at the table read. He quickly left to meet with other members of the team responsible for producing the episode.

Music Is Critical

One area in which MacFarlane takes a personal hand is the music for *Family Guy*. Perhaps more so than other cartoon shows, *Family Guy* places a great deal of emphasis on musical elements. On MacFarlane's insistence, Fox has provided *Family Guy* with a large budget for the production of music—for each episode, a fifty-six-piece orchestra is assembled. Similar animated shows may include music provided by a tiny combo of studio musicians.

As a child, MacFarlane played the trombone and piano and sang in school musicals; he still plays the piano daily. It was this background that led him to include musical numbers in all of his animated television programs—in addition to the shows' theme songs. MacFarlane's favorite Broadway musical is *The Sound of Music*—a poster of the movie version hangs over his desk. It is that type of broadly orchestrated, theatrical music that he sought to integrate into *Family Guy*.

Theme Song Sets the Tone

Family Guy's opening song-and-dance theme depicts the Griffin family participating in a costumed Broadway-style revue surrounded by dancers and orchestration. MacFarlane's musical tastes run beyond Broadway show tunes. He also enjoys American standards, jazz, and 1940s-era big band music.

His dedication to the musical aspects of the show was recognized in 2002 by his receipt of an Emmy Award—broadcast television's highest honor—for outstanding music and lyrics on *Family Guy*. Not merely a nice touch, musical numbers sprinkled throughout MacFarlane's animated television programs have a deliberate function: they lighten the otherwise heavy social messages embedded in the episodes.

Perhaps the biggest sensation created by a *Family Guy* musical homage occurred in 2007 when the show paid tribute to another of MacFarlane's favorite musicals, the 1960s-era Broadway play and film *The Music Man*. In the episode, Peter is a football player celebrating his touchdown by singing and dancing to the play's song "Shipoopi," which describes how to win a girl's affection. The next day curious fans flooded Google with questions about the meaning of the song's title. For a brief time *Shipoopi* was the search engine's top keyword search term.

Inside the Writers' Room

The music for *Family Guy* is just one aspect of the show's production in which MacFarlane's influence can be felt. Even his company name, Fuzzy Door Productions, is a nod to his college days when he lived in a residence with a distinctive-looking front door. The company logo was dreamed up by a former roommate, who captured the original door's 1970s-style fuzzy leopard print.

In the writers' room the show's writers can mull over their gags while standing at a vintage pinball machine. Providing illumination is a neon taproom sign: evidence of MacFarlane's boyish sense of humor.

MacFarlane's Cool Toys

When asked by a television interviewer to do so, Seth MacFarlane can do a spot-on imitation of Marty McFly, the teenage character portrayed by Michael J. Fox in the 1985 hit film *Back to the Future.* In the movie, McFly travels back in time and has to make sure his parents meet and fall in love. In the film, the time-travel device is a DeLorean, a silver, gull-winged sports car that had a brief production run and is highly sought by collectors today.

MacFarlane was just twelve years old when the film was released and says now the movie is among his favorites. With the wealth he has accumulated as one of Hollywood's most successful animators, MacFarlane has fulfilled a childhood dream to own a replica of the DeLorean driven by McFly. But his love of movie cars does not stop there. He also owns an Aston Martin, the British sports car driven by film spy James Bond. To MacFarlane—and Bond's other fans—the Aston Martin represents the essence of cool.

Besides the ability to afford high-end sports cars most movie fans would covet, MacFarlane's life has changed in other ways, thanks to his nearly twenty years in animation. The man who once wore the same shirt every day now dresses like a model and spray tans at work. He does not have a steady girlfriend, but he has dated a succession of beautiful actresses and models. And gone is the one-bedroom apartment he could barely afford, replaced by a $13 million gated mansion.

Tacked everywhere are hand-drawn images of characters who have appeared on the show but are no longer of use. According to Spencer Porter, MacFarlane's assistant, the drawings serve a purpose—to remind the staff not to include the characters in future shows.

The writers—including MacFarlane—produce a first draft of the show that runs more than the twenty-two minutes of animation time (the typical half-hour sitcom includes eight minutes of commercials and network promos.) Much of the script is crafted to sound as though it is improvised. To achieve that effect, writers speak the lines as they write them as though engaging in conversation with one another. "About half of the stuff that sounds improvised is already scripted, and we have to deliver it so it sounds like it was improvised," says MacFarlane. "The reason it works so well is because we let the writers do voices for the characters they have written, and it's kind of unique—few people ever notice it. . . . We base the animation around their own 'hums' and 'hahs,' rather than take them out."[26]

MacFarlane's goal is to continually take the show in directions fans least expect. Perhaps the biggest plot surprise the show has ever employed was killing off a main character. In a 2013 episode titled "The Life of Brian," the family dog is mortally wounded when he is run over by a car as he plays street hockey. The episode blew up on social media. Online petitions were posted to bring Brian back. "We were all very surprised, in a good way, that people still cared enough about that character to be that angry," MacFarlane says. "We thought it would create a little bit of a stir, but the rage wasn't something we counted on."[27] Working about a year ahead, the writers had simply written Brian out of three episodes, with plans to bring him back before the end of the season.

The scripts are rewritten several times—each print version of the script is color coded to define its position in the process. Each script runs through a reading, where the kinks are worked out and gags refined. Throughout the process, the scripts get shorter and the jokes sharper, until MacFarlane is satisfied with a final version that is recorded by the actors.

Following His Formula

Each *Family Guy* script bears MacFarlane's imprint, written under a formula he established when the show first premiered in 1999. The plot of each show relies less on a so-called linear story, in which each episode tells a story with a beginning and end. Rather, *Family Guy* episodes rely more on gags to tell the story. There is always something of a plot to the show, to be sure, but there are many detours that take viewers away from the plot as the writers slip in gag after gag. Essentially, the writers tell the story through a series of gags, rather than concocting a plot and then finding ways to make it funny.

After the script is completed, a storyboard is produced. This is a near scene-by-scene rendition of the show that resembles a comic strip. Artists work from the storyboard, providing sharper sketches and fleshing out the physical comedy that accompanies the spoken script. The initial storyboard is produced with ink and paper, but new technology enables artists to refine the sketches on computer screens; by using stylus pens, they can draw right on the screens. Unlike the old style of using ink and paper, though, the animator can combine the digital images to provide the first rough animation.

This rough version is then sent to the animatics department, where technicians match the dialogue recorded by the actors with the digital drawings. Essentially, the animatics department provides a rough cut of the show. After approvals by MacFarlane and the director, the rough cut is sent to the South Korean animation studio to complete the episode.

> "The idea [for *American Dad!*] was to do a current-day *All in the Family* that would be more political than *Family Guy,* with some attempt to balance the two sides as much as possible, which is difficult for us."[28]
>
> —*American Dad!* creator Seth MacFarlane.

American Dad!

It may seem as though MacFarlane's time is dominated by the production of *Family Guy*, but MacFarlane must also find time to devote himself to the production of *American Dad!*, the animated spy spoof whose staff shares office space with the staff of *Family Guy*. MacFarlane came up with the show idea in the early 2000s, developing it fully while *Family Guy* was off the air. He arrived at the premise almost accidentally while engaging in off-the-cuff political discussions with his staffers.

MacFarlane says, "My friends and I spent half our time complaining about President [George W.] Bush, and we figured, why don't we channel our anger into something creative. The idea was to do a current-day *All in the Family* that would be more political than *Family Guy*, with some attempt to balance the two sides as much as possible, which is difficult for us."[28]

Developed by veteran TV producer Norman Lear, *All in the Family* was a boundary-pushing prime-time comedy broadcast from 1971 to 1979. The show focused on the exploits of the Bunker family: blue-collar bigot, Archie; dim-witted wife, Edith; flower child daughter, Gloria; and politically radical son-in-law, Mike. Says MacFarlane:

> When I watch a rerun of *All in the Family* (which is quite often), I am blown away by its comic wizardry, by how far superior it is to any current network offerings. It endures because its creator was angry about injustice in the world: racism, sexism, homophobia, abuse of political power, economic disparity—the list goes on. In other words, angry about the right things.[29]

For his part, Lear, who is now in his nineties—far older than the typical fan of MacFarlane's comedy—praises the young animator. He says, "I can't think of anybody doing a better job right now of mining the foolishness of the human condition."[30]

All in the Family Influence

All in the Family, which spawned multiple spinoffs, made a star out of Carroll O'Connor, who played lead character Archie Bunker. Bunker, like Peter Griffin and *American Dad!* lead character Stan Smith, made outrageous comments as he exchanged verbal jabs with Edith, Gloria, and Mike. *All in the Family* viewers are very familiar with Archie's description of his son-in-law: "meathead."

> "I can't think of anybody doing a better job right now of mining the foolishness of the human condition."[30]
>
> —Norman Lear, producer of *All in the Family*.

In *American Dad!* MacFarlane cast his sister, Rachael, in the "meathead" role. She plays the Smiths' teenage daughter, Hayley, a strong woman whose liberal views often put her at odds with her conservative dad, a CIA agent.

When Fox launched *American Dad!*, the network once again went all out, giving it the prime spot immediately following the 2005 Super Bowl. The show ran for ten seasons on Fox before moving to TBS in 2014.

All in the Family *was a controversial yet popular television show in the 1970s. The Bunker family and their confrontations with and debates over racism, politics, and other social issues inspired Seth MacFarlane to create the biting political satire* American Dad!

MacFarlane serves as executive producer and was instrumental in designing the characters drawn by as many as fifty animators who work on the show. MacFarlane is a member of the writing team and provides the voice for Stan Smith and Roger, an extraterrestrial who is not allowed to leave the Smith house.

Cleveland Brown Goes It Alone

As MacFarlane looked for additional ideas for animated cartoons, it made sense for him to consider a *Family Guy* spinoff. In 2009, two years after the idea was first broached, he turned to Peter Griffin's drinking buddy, Cleveland Brown, and made him the star of his third

Mining 9/11 for Laughs

The emotions Americans feel about the September 11, 2001, terrorist attacks at the World Trade Center in New York City and Pentagon in Washington, DC, remain raw even today. While 9/11 is considered off-limits as a topic by many entertainers, Seth MacFarlane and *Family Guy* have felt no such restrictions. In a 2011 episode, Stewie and Brian travel back to 2001 to prevent the terrorist attacks. In doing so, however, they change the world in ways they had not intended, leading to another American civil war. Realizing their error, the two characters undo what they did, high-fiving themselves on their successful mission—failing to prevent the attacks that took the lives of some three thousand people.

Ironically, MacFarlane was supposed to have been a passenger on American Airlines Flight 11—the second airplane to strike the World Trade Center. MacFarlane missed the flight because he overslept that morning.

MacFarlane acknowledges that the 2001 terrorist attacks remain a sensitive topic among many people, but as a comedy writer he feels a responsibility to explore all events in modern culture—even those with tragic consequences—as sources of humor. He says, "After the fact, it was sobering, but people have a lot of close calls; you're crossing the street and you almost get hit by a car . . . this one just happened to be related to something massive. I really can't let that affect me because I'm a comedy writer. I have to put that in the back of my head."

Quoted in *Daily Mail* Reporter, "Have They Finally Crossed the Line? *Family Guy* Causes Outrage as Characters High-Five in Celebration of 9/11 Attacks," *Daily Mail* (London), November 15, 2011. www .dailymail.co.uk.

animated show, *The Cleveland Show*. For the new program, Cleveland, who had been one of *Family Guy*'s few African American characters, moved from Quahog, Rhode Island, to his original hometown of Stoolbend, Virginia, along with his fourteen-year-old son, Cleveland Jr. Once back home, he wed his high school sweetheart and formed a new family with her two children.

As with *American Dad!*, MacFarlane served as executive producer and worked on the writing team. He also gave voice to one of the characters, Tim the Bear—a neighbor of the show's protagonists, Cleveland and Donna Brown—who just happens to be a talking bear.

Polarizing Character

During the show's run Cleveland's ethnicity was always in the forefront. In the first episode, Peter Griffin, Cleveland's friend, expressed surprise that African American men cry; he thought they were capable only of anger.

Tom Shales, a critic from the *Washington Post*, had this to say about that type of joke in *The Cleveland Show*: "The humor doesn't necessarily promote racial stereotypes, but whenever a crude joke can be made out of it, Cleveland's race is mentioned—over and over, in scene after scene. The message that young viewers receive is that racial minorities are different, separate, apart from the norm."[31]

MacFarlane counters that it is better for a show to be polarizing—to offend some people—than to be pleasant and bland. "Cleveland is a polarizing character," he says. "People either love him or they're bored with him."[32]

The show lasted four seasons before its cancellation in 2013. Rather than abandoning the character, Cleveland returned to *Family Guy*, moving back to Quahog to resume his friendship with Peter. Meanwhile, the writers crafted jokes mostly focusing on Cleveland's failure to thrive on his own.

No Time to Be Sick

Even with the cancellation of *The Cleveland Show*, MacFarlane's insistence on maintaining a hand in virtually every aspect of his shows leaves him little time for leisure. "I don't get vacations," he says. "I once went for fifteen months, working seven days a week, and I put myself in the hospital, just from exhaustion."[33]

Because MacFarlane is so involved with his shows, particularly with *Family Guy*, when he is ill the tight production schedule gets backed up, ramping up the pressure even more. Even so, time away from work is rare. When he comes down with a cold, the characters he plays come down with a cold, too.

The fact that MacFarlane is willing to come to work with a head cold illustrates the dedication he brings to his work. It is the same level of professionalism he showed nearly twenty years ago when *Family Guy* premiered. Moreover, MacFarlane's commitment to the success of the show as well as his influence in the writers' room, animation studio, and recording studio are likely to continue for as long as *Family Guy* remains on the air.

CHAPTER THREE

MacFarlane Steps in Front of the Camera

For years audiences largely knew Seth MacFarlane by the characters he voiced on *Family Guy*—among them the wisecracking and guffawing Peter Griffin and the snide and devious baby Stewie. But that changed shortly after 11:30 p.m. on the night of September 16, 2012, when MacFarlane strode onto the stage of *Saturday Night Live* (*SNL*) to appear as guest host. On the air since 1975, *SNL* is television's most enduring comedy show. It provides audiences with cutting-edge political satire, irreverent humor, talented cast members, and the rare opportunity to see live performances. As the name suggests, *Saturday Night Live* is performed live. There are no retakes if a gag falls flat; for the show to be successful, the gags *have* to work.

By the time MacFarlane appeared on *SNL*, he had emerged as an enormously successful writer, voice actor, and animation producer, but he had not appeared before the camera or in front of a live audience since college. And so *SNL*'s venerable producer, Lorne Michaels, took a chance by recruiting MacFarlane to host the 2012–2013 season premiere—perhaps the most important show of the year for a series.

MacFarlane had been anxious to take on a project like hosting *SNL*. After nearly fifteen years of writing and producing animated shows, he felt it was time to broaden his career—to become more of a presence in front of the camera. "I tend to like to try things I haven't done before, for better or worse," he says. "I go into new things not afraid to fail. . . . I like things that scare me a little bit."[34]

A Hit on *SNL*

TV critics watched MacFarlane's performance carefully and, after the show aired, were in virtual agreement that MacFarlane had been a hit. Wrote *Rolling Stone* critic Logan Nicklaus, "MacFarlane was pitch-perfect as a sketch actor, clearly willing to commit to any and every character, whether in a deadpan role or an impression. He reached beyond the crutches of his signature voices and his sometimes sophomoric humor."[35]

Nicklaus and other critics lauded MacFarlane for one particular piece of acting: During *SNL*'s "Weekend Update" segment—a spoof of TV news broadcasts—MacFarlane appeared as Olympic swimmer Ryan Lochte and was interviewed by then *SNL* cast member Seth Meyers. (The broadcast aired just a few days following the completion of the 2012 Summer Olympics.) Dressed in a red warm-up suit, medals dangling from his neck, MacFarlane played Lochte as a confused meathead.

Leaning close to Meyers during the interview, MacFarlane's Lochte character said, "Hey Seth, do you wanna know a secret? If you hold your ear up to my ear you can hear the ocean."[36] For his part, Lochte complained that MacFarlane's characterization was unfair—he admitted that during an earlier part of his career he often stumbled through news interviews but now feels he holds his own while answering questions from reporters. Said Lochte, "I think they got me all wrong on there. The whole skit was from when I first started doing interviews like six or seven years ago. I didn't really know what to say doing interviews but now I'm more relaxed."[37] Still, Lochte took the ribbing in good fun and vowed to host *SNL* himself one day.

> "MacFarlane was pitch-perfect as a sketch actor, clearly willing to commit to any and every character, whether in a deadpan role or an impression. He reached beyond the crutches of his signature voices and his sometimes sophomoric humor."[35]
>
> —Logan Nicklaus, *Rolling Stone* critic.

Making His First Movie

MacFarlane's appearance on *SNL* was not the only sharp departure in a career devoted largely to animation and voice characterizations. Months before his appearance on *SNL*, MacFarlane's film *Ted* was

the first motion picture from the creator of
family guy

mark
wahlberg

mila
kunis

seth
macfarlane

ted

this summer

www.tedisreal.com

A movie poster for Ted *illustrates MacFarlane's intentions to combine childish innocence with comic irreverence. The successful film has grossed nearly $550 million worldwide since its release in 2012.*

released in June 2012. *Ted* was not an animated feature but rather a live-action comedy, although MacFarlane initially considered turning the idea into an animated television series. The film tells the story of John, a little boy who makes a wish—that his teddy bear would come to life. The wish is granted, and the toy bear—Ted—becomes the boy's best friend. But Ted remains the boy's closest companion even after John grows into adulthood. By now Ted is a wisecracking loafer who finds ways to disrupt the romantic life of his friend John, played by Mark Wahlberg, and John's girlfriend, played by Mila Kunis (who also provides the voice of *Family Guy* daughter Meg Griffin). MacFarlane says making the switch to movies was a way for him to shake off the Hollywood image that TV animators are entertainment lightweights. "There's a prejudice against the medium of animation," he says. "I don't care about winning awards, but it'll be nice to do something that is perceived as slightly more significant."[38]

In the R-rated movie—with greater tolerance for mature content—MacFarlane had fewer constraints than with his television shows. In the end, he observed, the movie he made would have been just the type his parents would have let him see when he was a child. "My parents were OK with me watching a lot of things when I was a kid, because they were around to explain. They swore, and they were very clear about what was right and wrong, but they didn't view bad language as the worst offense in the world. My mother would stub her toe and let loose a string of obscenities that you would not believe,"[39] MacFarlane says.

MacFarlane's fans were not disappointed by the content—the film contained an ample supply of lowbrow gags to keep the most devoted among them satisfied. Certainly, though, *Ted* found a wider audience than the usual *Family Guy* crowd: The film was a box-office smash, grossing more than $200 million, more than any other R-rated movie has ever made. Yet MacFarlane had no expectation that *Ted* would set records; as always, he went with his gut instinct on what he found entertaining, rather than trying to figure out what was likely to sell to a general audience.

> "There's a prejudice against the medium of animation. I don't care about winning awards, but it'll be nice to do something that is perceived as slightly more significant."[38]
>
> — *Family Guy* creator Seth MacFarlane.

Bringing Ted to Life

As an animator, it was only natural for Seth MacFarlane to bring an animated element to the motion picture comedy *Ted*. To achieve the animated teddy bear sequences that defined the movie, during production MacFarlane wore a motion-capture suit in a technique computer animators use to create lifelike characters. So when audiences saw a computer-animated teddy bear play the scenes alongside the actors, they were actually seeing MacFarlane, who not only provided the voice for Ted, but the motions for Ted's body as well. In fact, getting the computer-generated imaging (CGI) effects right was the biggest challenge he faced in directing the movie. Said MacFarlane:

> It always bugs me when I see a CGI character in movies and there's a pristine quality, a sense that this character is distanced from every other actor in the film. . . . I wanted to give Ted, the character, all of the same benefits that any traditional actor would have, and that meant doing the voice live on set with Mark [Wahlberg] and Mila [Kunis], and being mic'd the same way, so you don't feel like he's the one element that was inserted after the fact. That seems like such a simple and obvious approach. Everything had to be treated exactly as it would be treated for a live actor, and it really makes a huge difference; it really brings Ted into that world.

Quoted in Matt Barone, "Interview: Seth MacFarlane Talks *Ted*, Realistic CGI Characters, & Keeping *Family Guy* Relevant," *Complex*, June/July 2012. www.complex.com.

Critical Respect at Last

There is little doubt that he was not expecting approval from someone like veteran film critic Rex Reed, who wrote, "Most of *Ted* eludes description, analysis and explanation. You just have to hold onto your own certifiable sense of humor and let Mr. MacFarlane take you where he wants to go. Then get out of the way and enjoy it. Will it make you wince with embarrassment? That's a promise. Will you also laugh? In double-time."[40]

Another longtime critic who liked the movie was Roger Ebert. He wrote:

What's remarkable about *Ted* is that it doesn't run out of steam. MacFarlane seems unwilling to stop after the first pay-off of a scene. He keeps embellishing. In *Ted*, he has an inexhaustible source of socially obnoxious behavior and language, and it's uncanny the way a teddy bear can get away with doing and saying things we wouldn't necessarily accept from a human character.[41]

Not so smitten was A.O. Scott, a movie critic for the *New York Times*, who found MacFarlane a talentless director. He wrote:

There are some genuinely, wildly funny bits in the movie: a brutal motel-room fistfight between Ted and John; a cocaine-fueled talking binge; a few choice insults and smutty riffs but the feature film is not a hospitable form for Mr. MacFarlane. He has no particular visual knack, little interest in storytelling and nothing better to do with his naughty bear besides stuff him into a soft, sentimental comedy that seems almost proud of its lack of wit or conviction.[42]

Peter, Ted, or Brian

Nicole Sperling of the *Los Angeles Times* noted that Ted's voice sounded a lot like the voice of Peter Griffin from *Family Guy*. She wrote:

Of course, both are voiced by writer-director Seth MacFarlane, so it's easy to understand why they are so alike. Or is it? MacFarlane also voices *Family Guy*'s baby Stewie, the dog Brian, and the next-door neighbor Quagmire, and all three have completely different accents. MacFarlane said he tried to find a voice for Ted that would be distinct from Griffin's Rhode Island dialect, but was challenged by the task from the very beginning. MacFarlane felt bound to his own New England roots. He said, "As I was coming up with the voice for Ted, I kept trying to veer away. I finally said, 'He's a Boston guy, and this is me doing a Boston accent,' which is not that far removed from me doing a Rhode Island accent for Peter. It is what it is."[43]

For his part, MacFarlane perceives some vocalization differences between Ted and Peter. In fact, he says the voice he has given Ted reminds him more of what Brian would sound like with a Boston accent. In addition to providing the voice of Ted, as with *Family Guy*, MacFarlane was involved in virtually all facets of the film's production. He directed the film and also headed the writing team. When MacFarlane first envisioned the character of Ted, he pictured a raggedy bear that had perhaps been too well loved. He subsequently changed his mind. MacFarlane says, "When I wrote the first draft of the outline he was going to be missing an ear, he was going to be missing an eye, there was going to be stuffing coming out and stains. It got to the point where he wasn't going to be cute anymore, so I toned it down."[44]

> "Seth MacFarlane is getting a bad rap from critics who can't take a joke. [As host of the Oscars,] he was risky . . . and riotous . . . a breath of fresh air to an otherwise safe awards show."[48]
>
> —Carole Lieberman, Los Angeles psychiatrist.

Hosting the Academy Awards

Months after the release of *Ted* as well as his *SNL* appearance, MacFarlane's career took an even riskier turn when he agreed to host the annual telecast of the Academy Awards. One of the entertainment world's premier events, each year the "Oscars" awards show draws tens of millions of viewers—the February 2013 telecast featuring MacFarlane as host recorded a US television audience of some 40 million. Those numbers were good enough to make MacFarlane's turn at helming the show one of the most watched in the previous six years. Worldwide, the show garnered an estimated audience of 1 billion or more viewers.

Seth MacFarlane hosted the Academy Awards show in 2013. Some viewers and Hollywood insiders were put off by MacFarlane's cheeky wit and off-color jokes, but others defended MacFarlane by pointing out that the Academy had known his reputation for mockery.

The Academy Awards telecast is a variety show featuring live performances of the songs nominated for Oscars, film clips from the nominated movies, and speeches by the winners. Holding it all together is the host, who opens the show with a comedic monologue and then pops onto the stage from time to time to introduce segments, interact with the stars, and find ways to keep the audience engaged—and laughing. Preparing for the Academy Awards telecast took Mac-Farlane more than six months, and provided him with some tense moments when he came down with the flu only three weeks before the show; multiple visits to the doctor were needed, as were postponements of his song-and-dance rehearsals and monologue refinements.

MacFarlane decided to attack the Academy Awards gig with the same irreverence and potty-style humor that he brings to all his projects. During the three-hour telecast, MacFarlane made jokes mocking women, racial and ethnic groups, and gays, among others. In the opening moments of the show, MacFarlane launched into a song parodying actresses who have bared their breasts on film—among them some of Hollywood's biggest stars. As with most of what MacFarlane does, the song prompted complaints from those who did not find humor in the performance. Critics pointed out that in most cases, the roles played by those actresses were not intended to display partial nudity for gratuitous purposes, but rather to portray characters in the throes of emotional conflicts or even during scenes of sexual violence. Said film producer Elizabeth Cantillon:

> I was with a number of women in the movie business who were shocked that that's what the Academy Awards chose to emphasize when really what we should be doing is promoting growth to our business and what's great about our business.
>
> You're talking about the great American actresses, you're talking about Angelina Jolie and Meryl Streep. People who have had long and successful careers, have won awards, and objectifying them and it's not right—even if you're trying to be humorous it's identifying a select group and picking on them for ridicule.[45]

Under the Microscope

Other critics suggested MacFarlane was simply not a good fit for the Oscars telecast. The Academy Awards audience is usually made up of older, more mature viewers, rather than the fans who can be counted among *Family Guy* viewers. Clearly, many of the people sitting in the Dolby Theater in Los Angeles where the show is produced were in no mood for MacFarlane's brand of humor. Said Thelma Adams, an editor for Yahoo! Movies, "Watch an episode of *Family Guy* and you'll know it's not a good match for Hollywood honchos sitting in stiff chairs in tuxes and tiaras. . . . [They are] a tough and tense crowd."[46]

But many in Hollywood came to MacFarlane's defense, including Neil Meron, who produced the Academy Awards telecast. He said:

> Seth is irreverent, he comments on things that happen in our culture, and that's what he did and we thought he did an extraordinary job. People have complained for years and years that the Oscars were becoming irrelevant. And I think what

we did this year is to really make them part of the cultural conversation, and I think that's the important part that people will take away.[47]

Another MacFarlane defender was Los Angeles psychiatrist Carole Lieberman, who often offers commentary on the media. She said, "Seth MacFarlane is getting a bad rap from critics who can't take a joke. He was risky . . . and riotous . . . a breath of fresh air to an otherwise safe awards show."[48]

Joking About Hitler

As for MacFarlane, if he felt scorched by the criticism, he did not show signs of backing down. He knew going in that critics were unlikely to sing his praises. During the Oscars telecast, MacFarlane made a gag about one of the nominees—the film *Amour*, which was produced by filmmakers in Germany and Austria. During the telecast, MacFarlane quipped, "The last time Austria and Germany got together and co-produced something it was Hitler, but this is much better."[49]

Making a joke about Adolf Hitler, one of history's cruelest dictators, prompted widespread criticism from newspaper columnists, TV commentators, and Hollywood celebrities, but MacFarlane shrugged it off.

In addition to serving as host for the Oscars, MacFarlane was a nominee for cowriting "Everybody Needs a Best Friend," the theme song from *Ted*. The song—written from the perspective of a teddy bear—was recorded by MacFarlane's friend, singer Norah Jones. The song did not win the Oscar. It lost to the featured song in the James Bond thriller *Skyfall*. As for MacFarlane, he admits he was shocked even to have been in the running. He says, "It's so ingrained in me that 'Oh, we must be hated by everybody.' So it's become this sort of inability to process any kind of positive feedback. We all focus on the negative, you know."[50]

Down and Out in the West

A year after MacFarlane's appearance on the Academy Awards telecast stirred controversy, he released his second live-action film,

A Love of Big Band Music

When it comes to music, Seth MacFarlane is blissfully out of step with the times. Ever since high school he has been a fan of music from the 1940s, taking his inspiration from iconic crooner Frank Sinatra, film director Woody Allen, and the vinyl albums he listened to from his grandfather's record collection. One of America's most prolific movie directors and known for his comedies, Allen is a musician, composer, stand-up comic, and writer who puts a lot of thought into the music he incorporates into his films. *Radio Days*, which is loosely based on Allen's Brooklyn childhood in the days before television, featured forty-three songs from that era. MacFarlane recalls:

> When I was a kid in high school, my cousin got me into Woody Allen. I saw *Radio Days,* which was a wonderful platform for music in the '40s and I hunted down more of it. Then I discovered the music of the '50s, which is the golden era of big-band orchestration. You get a little more experimentation and richness. . . . One of the reasons that nothing really hits me in the gut in contemporary music is that there are just too few instrumentalists. [In big-band music] if you take vocals out of the track, you have orchestrations that are ingenious works of art. That just doesn't happen anymore.

MacFarlane has performed in top venues such as Carnegie Hall in New York and the Royal Albert Hall in London. He has recorded two albums. To make *Music Is Better than Words*, MacFarlane used the same microphone Sinatra used, and like him, was recorded while singing in front of a fifty-five-piece orchestra. A second album, *Holiday for Swing*, features holiday tunes and was released in 2014.

Quoted in David Ng, "Seth MacFarlane Is a Singing Guy Too," *Los Angeles Times,* March 23, 2011. http://articles.latimes.com.

A Million Ways to Die in the West. The film represents still another step in the evolution of his entertainment career. In *Ted*, MacFarlane was a presence on the screen—but he was not actually on the screen. With *A Million Ways to Die in the West*, MacFarlane also took a starring role in the comedy. And typical of a MacFarlane production, he also wrote and directed the film.

In *A Million Ways to Die in the West*, set in 1882, MacFarlane plays the main character, Albert Stark. After refusing to participate in a gunfight, Stark struggles to win back the affections of his girlfriend Anna, played by Charlize Theron. As a fan of Westerns, MacFarlane thought audiences would appreciate a funny, updated look at the Old West. He spent four years working on *A Million Ways to Die in the West* only to discover that his normally on-target instincts had missed

A promotional poster for A Million Ways to Die in the West. *Though the film was popular with MacFarlane's core fans, the movie did not receive much critical praise, nor did it perform particularly well at the box office.*

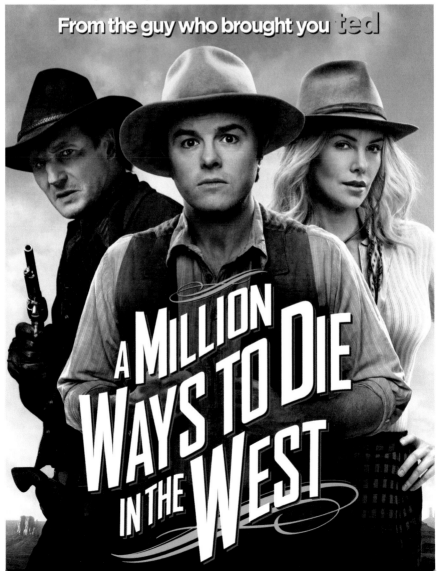

the mark. The film represented another twist in MacFarlane's career: For the first time since he entered the entertainment business, Mac-Farlane found both critics and fans cold to the production.

Critics praised the performances of A-list stars such as Liam Neeson, Amanda Seyfried, and Neil Patrick Harris, but many also found MacFarlane's talent as an actor lacking. "MacFarlane, the *Family Guy* creator, controversial one-time Oscar host, and writer-director of the gleefully, talking-plush-toy comedy *Ted*, makes his first mistake casting himself in the lead," wrote Steven Rea, film critic for the *Philadelphia Inquirer*. Rea added, "Before this way-too-long endeavor heads off into the proverbial sunset, its slew of gags about excrement (human, equine, ruminant mammals), intestinal gasses, bodily fluids, sex and genitalia is augmented by truly offensive bits at the expense of blacks and women."[51]

The script was typical MacFarlane—jokes centered on flatulence and bodily fluids while African Americans and women shouldered their share of comical abuse. But Rea said most of the gags fell flat. "It's beyond bad taste," he wrote. "It's just bad."[52]

Another critic, Rick Bentley of the *Fresno Bee*, said that as a director MacFarlane was guilty of letting the jokes in *A Million Ways to Die in the West* outstay their welcome. However, Bentley did hold out some hope that MacFarlane could one day be held in the same esteem as veteran comedic director and funnyman Mel Brooks, whose own western, *Blazing Saddles*, is considered a movie classic. Bentley wrote, "If MacFarlane ever corrects his bad habits as a director, he could become the Mel Brooks of the 21st century—quirky, weird, and often outrageous. The big difference, as so blatantly shown in this film, is that he never knows when to move on from a joke, often leaving it to die a slow death or go from smart to juvenile."[53]

Evidence suggests all but MacFarlane's most devoted fans passed on the film. The movie grossed $42 million—just $2 million more than its production cost and less than a quarter of what *Ted* had earned. Yet whether *A Million Ways to Die in the West* is perceived as a win or a loss in MacFarlane's column may not be so important in the end. After all, MacFarlane is never happier than when he is risking failure by trying something new, and nothing has made him more vulnerable to media criticism than stepping out in front of the camera.

CHAPTER FOUR

Expanding His Fan Base

I n *A Million Ways to Die in the West*, Seth MacFarlane had a lot of fun lampooning old movie westerns. In *Ted*, MacFarlane's film was essentially a parody of buddy comedies, only in this case the buddies were a guy and his teddy bear. And in shows like *Family Guy* and *American Dad!*, MacFarlane has found a lot of laughs poking fun at life in middle-class suburban America. Along the way he has found humor in serious issues such as AIDS, sexual violence, and abortion—topics that are often considered too inflammatory to be the butt of jokes. But MacFarlane has never shied away from lampooning subjects that range from the sacred to the ridiculous, and the overall success of his projects leads him to believe that there is an audience for all types of humor.

In *Bordertown*, MacFarlane's animated series scheduled to premiere in 2015, the veteran producer will attempt to mine laughs in one of America's most emotional and divisive issues: immigration. There is little question that by the second decade of the twenty-first century, few issues have sparked as much debate and furor than what to do about the more than 11 million illegal immigrants, most from Mexico and other Latin American countries, who have found homes in the United States.

MacFarlane has, in fact, already waded into the immigration debate by criticizing Arizona's so-called Papers Please law. Adopted by the Arizona legislature in 2010, the law gives police officers the right to stop people they suspect of being illegal aliens and demand to see their driver's license or another form of identification. "It's too much. It's kind of a slap in the face, it's not the way to handle it," MacFarlane said shortly after the law was passed. "Nobody but the Nazis ever asked anybody for their papers. . . . Walking down the street, a cop can come up to you and say 'May I see your papers?'—I think they should be required to ask that question in German if the law sticks around."[54]

Critics of the law suggested it is enforced through the practice of racial profiling—identifying suspects solely on the basis of belonging to a certain group. Civil rights groups contested the law in court, but in 2012 the US Supreme Court let the law stand, ensuring that the commentary and criticism would continue.

The furor over Arizona's Papers Please law illustrates the level of emotion that accompanies the immigration issue in American society. But as MacFarlane has demonstrated in the past, just because a topic stirs emotion and is the subject of serious debate does not mean it cannot be made the subject of comedy. Says Lalo Alcaraz, a writer MacFarlane has enlisted for *Bordertown*:

> "I think some of the Latino audience [for *Bordertown*] will be very pleased by seeing a realistic kind of take on realistic characters that the Latino characters will show. And then some will say it's just promoting stereotypes and they'll close their mind."[55]
>
> —Lalo Alcaraz, *Bordertown* writer.

> It's going to be pretty cutting edge for any television show, and everyone's feathers will be ruffled because everyone gets it. There are no sacred cows, really. I think some of the Latino audience will be very pleased by seeing a realistic kind of take on realistic characters that the Latino characters will show. And then some will say it's just promoting stereotypes and they'll close their mind.[55]

Touchy Relationship

Fox has held the rights to *Bordertown* since 2009 but had been waiting for the proper slot in which to schedule the show. Fox was able to find a slot for *Bordertown* on Sunday evenings because the network decided not to renew *American Dad!* for 2015. (The show did not leave the airwaves—the adventures of agent Stan Smith and family have moved to TBS.) Moreover, with immigration controversies constantly in the news, Fox executives found the time right to launch *Bordertown*.

A half-hour series, *Bordertown* will focus on the misadventures of Ernesto Gonzalez and his family—legal Mexican American immigrants living in a Texas town near the Mexican border. A key part of the story will feature Gonzalez's touchy relationship with his next-

Protestors in Phoenix, Arizona, demonstrate against the 2012 US Supreme Court decision to uphold the state's right to demand proof of immigration status from anyone stopped by police. Seth MacFarlane used the resulting heightened tensions and emotions as a source of humor for Bordertown.

door neighbor, Bud Buckwald, a US Border Patrol agent. Gonzalez is optimistic and unflappable, and he seeks only to fit into American society. Buckwald, on the other hand, is bigoted, suspicious, and short-tempered.

While the plot for *Bordertown* may seem to reflect a scenario more suited to high drama, MacFarlane's fans can be assured it will be produced with comedy in mind. Plenty of *Family Guy*–style gags are planned for the show—meaning MacFarlane hopes the millions of devoted Griffin family fans will tune in.

Lagging in Latino Viewership

Fox also hopes a lot of Latino viewers will tune in as well. According to US Census figures, the Latino population stood at about 54 million in 2013 and is expected to grow to 60 million by 2020. By then Latinos will make up nearly 20 percent of the US population. But Latinos make up a small portion of the Fox audience—the network trails other American networks in Latino viewership, according to Statista, a New York–based market research company. Fox's Latino viewership in 2014 averaged just some 385,000 viewers per day. In contrast, ABC drew more than 600,000 Latino viewers per day, while NBC recorded 480,000 and CBS, 430,000.

Given such a dismal viewership among Latinos, Fox executives are clearly banking on their edgiest animator to raise the network's viewership among Latino Americans. Latinos who tune in to *Bordertown* will find the talents of Latino voice artists, writers, and animators who will help bring life to the Gonzalez family and ensure there will be plenty for Latinos to laugh about. Says Lucas Molandes, a Latino comedian and contributor to the entertainment website Tú Vez (Your Time):

> One definite mark in the plus column for *Bordertown* is that the show's producers . . . have hired Lalo Alcaraz to write for *Bordertown*. . . . The cynic in me can't help but feel the hiring of Alcaraz was a political move by the show's creators to provide some kind of legitimacy to the show. . . . The optimist in me hopes that Lalo will be allowed to bring heart and intelligence to the characters in *Bordertown*, which will give viewers something of substance to take away. And I hope the trend of hiring Latino writers continues in the upward direction.[56]

Speaking Out for Those Who Cannot

Alcaraz, a Mexican American cartoonist and writer, was one of the first Latino talents MacFarlane drafted for the show. Since 2002 Alcaraz has written and drawn *La Cucaracha* ("The Cockroach"), which is published in nearly one hundred Sunday newspapers in America. *La Cucaracha* has been described as a Latino version of *Doonesbury*, the longtime newspaper comic strip that finds a lot of humor in politics and social issues.

Alcaraz ought to feel right at home with the type of criticism *Bordertown* is likely to engender from some viewers and television critics. Since its debut *La Cucaracha* has been highly critical of the American government's policy toward immigration. Moreover, like MacFarlane, Alcaraz is not above resorting to gutter humor to make his point. In 2007 the *Houston Chronicle* dropped the comic strip after Alcaraz started using profanity in the language uttered by his characters. Like MacFarlane, Alcaraz stands by his humor and sees no reason to back down—particularly when it comes to the immigration question. "I saw how we were all treated as a kid," says Alcaraz, who grew up in San Diego, California, a city that borders Mexico. "We were at a different caste level. I didn't like it, and I grew up angry wondering why am I angry? And then I finally figured it out and got to speak out about it. What's right is right, and as an artist you're supposed to do the right thing and help those who can't speak."[57]

If *Bordertown* turns out to be a hit, it is sure to help fuel people's passions about immigration. "I know it's just a cartoon," says Alcaraz. "But if you know me, you know how I feel about cartoons. They are super important! Cartoons have allowed me to tell truths, to pick fights with the privileged, the greedy and the stupid."[58]

Of course, this *is* a MacFarlane production—which means MacFarlane-style comedy. According to Alcaraz, there will be plenty of gags about flatulence, sex, and ethnic groups—in other words, typical MacFarlane fare. Alcaraz says that during the course of planning the show, he met with a group of US Border Patrol agents. "I said imagine *Family Guy* with Mexicans in it and their eyes lit up," he says. "I'm not sure they'll like the portrayal of the Border Patrol but we'll see."[59]

A photo of Lalo Alcaraz working on his comic strip La Cucaracha *in 2004. Seth MacFarlane hired Alcaraz to write for* Bordertown, *knowing that the Mexican-born artist is critical of US immigration policy and willing to use crude humor in making his arguments clear.*

Delegating Responsibilities

Alcaraz is not the only Latino who has been drafted to work on *Bordertown*. In fact, more than half of the show's characters will be voiced by Latino actors, many of them immigrants from Mexico. In addition, a third of the writing staff is composed of Latinos. It is believed to be the first time in the history of American television that such a large percentage of a show's cast and creative staff are composed of Latinos.

Honored by Harvard

As an animator, producer, voice artist, and writer, Seth MacFarlane is rarely ranked in the same company as members of Congress, scientists, and proponents of human rights. But in 2011 he found himself named the recipient of an award that in the past had gone only to those types of achievers. MacFarlane was named Harvard Humanist of the Year by the Harvard Humanist Chaplaincy. A humanist is a person who views the world through the prism of science and rational thought and usually does not believe in God. MacFarlane is an atheist.

In making its selection, the chaplaincy observed that it usually selects recipients older than MacFarlane but felt compelled to choose him based on his unwavering support of science and social justice issues such as gay rights. Both *American Dad!* and *Family Guy* have featured sympathetic story lines addressing gay marriage and the adoption of children by gay couples.

The award was presented to MacFarlane in a church, an ironic location given that he often makes jokes about blind adherence to religious faith in his animated programs.

One of the actors who will be featured on *Bordertown* is Nicholas Gonzalez, who has appeared in a semiregular role as detective Luke Morales on the Fox supernatural drama *Sleepy Hollow*. On *Bordertown*, Gonzalez gives voice to Ernesto Gonzalez as well as to his nephew J.C., a recent college graduate and loudmouth political liberal. Another character Gonzalez will voice is that of a criminal named Pablo Barracuda.

Gonzalez has very little experience as a voice actor—before *Bordertown* his lone voice role was as a scary drug lord in a single episode of the animated series *BoJack Horseman*, a Netflix-produced comedy that lasted a single season. Viewers of *Bordertown* will find Gonzalez providing a high, squeaky voice for Ernesto and a gruff, no-funny-business voice for Pablo. "They're super-distinct," he says. "Closest to my own voice is J.C.—the annoying, proselytizing liberal."[60]

Familiar Voices

The cast also features some voices familiar to many TV viewers. Hank Azaria, best known for providing many voices on *The Simpsons*—including Moe the bartender, convenience store owner Apu, and police chief Clancy Wiggum—will give voice to border agent Bud Buckwald. Playing Janice, Bud's wife, is Alex Borstein, who also voices Lois Griffin on *Family Guy*. Borstein also provides the voice for the Buckwald's insecure daughter, Becky, while comic actor Judah Friedlander plays son Sanford—a character who thinks he is cooler than he really is. Rounding out the Buckwald family is Gert (portrayed by Missi Pyle), a five-year-old whose constant companion is a pet pig.

Bordertown will certainly have the look and feel of a Seth Mac-Farlane production—MacFarlane's company, Fuzzy Door Productions, is producing the show, and MacFarlane has assumed the role of executive producer. Nevertheless, *Bordertown* will mark a sharp departure from other MacFarlane-produced projects in that by late 2014 he had not yet been listed as a voice actor for the show. Nor is he serving on the writing team.

MacFarlane says he has reached the point in his career when he must be prepared to delegate responsibilities to others. He says:

> I'm a big believer in hiring people who are smarter than you are. That's one of the things that has made it all work. The importance of *Family Guy* is always paramount—that's a show that really does still have to be taken care of in a big way. . . . I'm surrounded by a team of people who I can really delegate to in a big way. It becomes a matter of relinquishing the vision to somebody you trust on a day-to-day basis, and they do a fantastic job. It makes it unnecessary for me to have to juggle eight million things at the same time, which I really couldn't do. I wouldn't enjoy it, it would be impossible, and I'd drop dead from exhaustion.[61]

Blunt Talk

Part of the reason MacFarlane will find it necessary to let others run the day-to-day business of *Bordertown* is that he has many other projects under development. Indeed, as *Bordertown* hits the airwaves, another MacFarlane production is scheduled to premiere as well. Titled *Blunt Talk*, the show will not be animated but is rather a live-action situation comedy that centers on the career of Walter Blunt, a British TV personality who crosses the Atlantic to star in an American cable TV interview show.

Starring as Blunt is Patrick Stewart, a veteran British actor known largely to American audiences for his role as Professor Charles Xavier in the popular *X-Men* series of action films and for portraying captain Jean-Luc Picard in the *Star Trek: The Next Generation* TV series. But he is also familiar to MacFarlane fans because he provides the voice of CIA deputy director Avery Bullock on the *American Dad!* series.

Blunt Talk will mark something of a departure for MacFarlane because it will not feature the slapstick-style comedy common in *Family Guy* or even MacFarlane's live-action features, such as *Ted*. Instead, *Blunt Talk* will mine laughs from the dialogue among the characters as well as the socially uncomfortable situations in which the characters find themselves.

There is no question that there is a lot of grist for laughs in the show. Blunt will deal with dysfunctional network bosses, incompetent staff members, and several ex-wives, all of whom complicate his life. Certainly, critics are anticipating some lowbrow humor—this is, after all, a MacFarlane production. But unlike *Family Guy*, the show will not be written as a series of gags strung together. Instead, it will rely more heavily on its plotlines. Each show will tell a story—with the gags added *after* the plot is worked out.

Says Stewart, "When we meet Blunt his show is no longer doing well, the numbers are dreadful and his career is in crisis. . . . He just keeps falling into these tailspins. One after another. It's completely realistic and truthful. This is not a gag show, it's not one-liners."[62] The Starz cable network has made a two-year commitment to *Blunt Talk*, ordering shows for the 2015 and 2016 seasons.

Back into the Cosmos

Regardless of where they find their laughs, *Bordertown* and *Blunt Talk* are comedies that are the type of content viewers have come to expect from MacFarlane-produced entertainment. But in 2014 MacFarlane showed he does have a serious side when he produced the documentary series *Cosmos: A Spacetime Odyssey*. Airing simultaneously on Fox and the National Geographic Channel, the thirteen-episode series celebrated science and discovery, helping viewers understand the mysteries of evolution and development of life on Earth, the motions of the planets, the speed of light, and the properties of magnets, among other topics. It was hosted by astronomer Neil deGrasse Tyson.

The 2014 series was actually an updated version of a 1980 series, *Cosmos: A Personal Voyage*, that aired on PBS and was hosted by astronomer Carl Sagan. The author of several books on astronomy and space science, Sagan died in 1996, but his wife, Ann Druyan, always kept alive the idea of reviving the series. MacFarlane met Druyan in 2008 while attending an event at the Los Angeles headquarters of the National Academy of Sciences and agreed then to pursue the idea of reviving the series.

MacFarlane watched the old Sagan series as a boy and, as he grew older, read several of Sagan's books. After speaking more with Druyan as well as Tyson, MacFarlane committed to a reboot of *Cosmos*. As the series aired in the spring of 2014, it received high marks from TV critics. Wrote David Wiegand, TV critic for the *San Francisco Chronicle*, "Tyson achieves what Sagan did, though: making science fun and interesting even for people who wouldn't know an igneous rock from a composite, but without either talking down to his audience or making them think they're being held against their will in a postgraduate physics lecture."[63]

The show found a large audience—an average of 3 million viewers tuned in for each episode. *Cosmos* went on to win a dozen Emmy Awards as well as other honors, including the Critics' Choice Television Award for Best Reality Series. As for MacFarlane, he welcomed the praise—proving to his critics that he can provide the public with more than just Peter Griffin–style gags. "I like the fact that I haven't

> "When we meet Blunt [in the show *Blunt Talk*] his show is no longer doing well, the numbers are dreadful and his career is in crisis. . . . He just keeps falling into these tailspins. One after another. It's completely realistic and truthful."[62]
>
> —Patrick Stewart, the actor portraying Walter Blunt.

Astrophysicist Neil deGrasse Tyson (center) and producer Seth MacFarlane (second from right) join a panel of other producers of Cosmos: A Spacetime Odyssey. The 2014 series explored major scientific concepts and demonstrated MacFarlane's interest in developing more serious programs.

shoehorned myself into one M.O. [modus operandi, or way of doing things]," says MacFarlane. "I like the fact that *Family Guy* and *Cosmos* exist at the same time. It makes things fun."[64]

Following the conclusion of the series in June 2014, stories surfaced in the entertainment media suggesting that Tyson would like to return for a second season of *Cosmos*. Moreover, in December 2014, MacFarlane and Tyson both confirmed on their Twitter feeds that they are in discussions to produce a second season of *Cosmos* episodes. If a second season is ultimately produced, though, due to the extensive time it would take to write and produce the series, it may take a few years before it debuts on network TV. Says Tyson, "We're all flattered that people are thinking [about a second season] but it's not clear that this was the kind of content you want to rattle off one year after the next."[65]

Film and Theater Projects

MacFarlane began discussions with Tyson about producing a new season of *Cosmos* as he completed postproduction work on his much-anticipated sequel to *Ted*. Titled *Ted 2*, the film is slated for release in the summer of 2015. Mark Wahlberg returns as John, and MacFarlane reprises the voice of Ted (and he will be wearing the motion-capture suit again to bring his physical presence to the computer-animated toy bear).

Once again, John finds Ted entangled in his romantic life as he struggles to maintain his friendship with his lifelong companion as well as a relationship with a new girlfriend, played by Amanda Seyfried. Along the way there will be plenty of lowbrow gags like those audiences found appealing in the original hit film from 2012. Similarities aside, though, MacFarlane has said that he would not be happy if he were merely making a rehash of the first film. So this time around audiences can expect to see some new areas of Ted's life explored. One of those is likely to involve Ted having a legal problem that requires him to hire a civil rights lawyer, portrayed by Morgan Freeman.

Another film idea that has been talked about for years—mostly by MacFarlane fans in the blogosphere—is a full-length *Family Guy* movie. MacFarlane acknowledges that although there are no immediate plans to bring the exploits of the Griffin family to movie screens, a *Family Guy* movie is a possibility at some point. "I have an idea of what it would be, but I just never had the time," he says. "I spent so many years working on the show seven days a week that the urge to try other things was so strong. It's not on my immediate list of things to do, but I would be shocked if it never happened."[66]

Given his interest in Broadway-style dance and music, MacFarlane has also expressed interest in writing a Broadway musical—and there is precedent for TV animators making the transition to the stage. In 2011 the hit musical comedy *The Book of Mormon* debuted on Broadway. The play, which won the Tony Award for Best Musical—Broadway's highest

> "I like the fact that I haven't shoehorned myself into one M.O. I like the fact that *Family Guy* and *Cosmos* exist at the same time. It makes things fun."[64]
>
> —*Family Guy* creator Seth MacFarlane.

Did Seth MacFarlane Steal the Idea for *Ted*?

A street-smart, cigarette-smoking teddy bear hangs out on a couch with his human friends making jokes and engaging in frat-boy behavior. Sounds like the lead character in Seth MacFarlane's blockbuster movie *Ted*, but it also describes the character Charlie the Abusive Teddy Bear. Charlie briefly had his own television show in 1996 before going on to star in the Internet series *Acting School Academy* in 2008. More than 1 million viewers reportedly watched Charlie's antics on websites such as YouTube and Funny or Die.

Charlie is the creation of the California animation company Bengal Mangle Productions, which in 2014 filed a lawsuit in US District Court in Los Angeles accusing MacFarlane, Universal Pictures, and Fuzzy Door Productions of infringing on its copyright for the animated bear. In other words, Bengal Mangle alleges that MacFarlane used its character without permission. In the lawsuit, Bengal Mangle points out that the two bears share a common Twitter style. For example, Charlie tweeted: "I have a mission and it is to drink." And Ted tweeted: "I drink on Tuesday night to celebrate the fact that it ain't Monday night."

By late 2014 a decision on Bengal Mangle's complaint had not been made, and the lawsuit had not deterred MacFarlane or his partners from going ahead with the *Ted* sequel.

Quoted in Alan Duke, "Lawsuit: Seth MacFarlane's *Ted* Ripped off *Charlie the Abusive Bear*," CNN, July 17, 2014. www.cnn.com.

honor—was conceived and produced by Trey Parker and Matt Stone, the producers of the oddball animated comedy *South Park*.

Broadway producer Neil Meron, who was instrumental in convincing MacFarlane to host the Academy Awards telecast, says MacFarlane has what it takes to make it on Broadway. "That would be a dream come true," Meron says. "The furthest thing from our conversations right now is for Seth to do a Broadway musical, but it's a great idea."[67]

Humor in Unexpected Places

When *Family Guy* ends its run, MacFarlane says he will search for new projects that stir his creative juices and keep his insecurity at bay. He says:

> I still don't know if I'm funny. I operate, as a lot of comedy writers do, on insecurity in what I am doing. There are negatives to that and positives to that. The positive is that if you are not sure you're good, you push yourself 100 times harder to be good. Sometimes you get there. Don't get me wrong, I'm confident in the shows and in the shows as comedy entities. But I'm still in the writer's room every day of the week pitching "jokes" I'm not sure have any merit to them. I'm always going for the kill without knowing if my gun is loaded.[68]

In a career that has now spanned some twenty years dating back to 1996 when he joined Hanna-Barbera as an animator, MacFarlane has established himself not only as a highly successful animator but also as a film and TV producer who is not hesitant about leaving his cartoon world comfort zone. In the meantime, he has helped make potty jokes acceptable to the Hollywood establishment, turned Peter Griffin into one of the country's most recognizable goofballs, made people believe teddy bears can talk, and above all, proved that humor can be found in the most unexpected places.

SOURCE NOTES

Introduction: Humor on the Edge

1. Quoted in International Movie Database, "*Family Guy*: Death Has a Shadow," 2014. www.imdb.com.
2. Seth MacFarlane, interview by Rob Tannenbaum, "Seth MacFarlane: September 2009," in *50 Years of the Playboy Interview*. Beverly Hills: Playboy Enterprises, 2012, eBook.
3. Quoted in Tannenbaum, "Seth MacFarlane."
4. Quoted in Dan Snierson, "Best Crossover Ever," *Entertainment Weekly*, September 12, 2014, p. 30.

Chapter One: Born to Cartoon

5. Quoted in IGN Filmforce, "An Interview with Seth MacFarlane," July 21, 2003. www.ign.com.
6. Quoted in Claire Hoffman, "No. 1 Offender," *New Yorker*, June 18, 2012, p. 38.
7. Bruce Newman, "Young, Talented, Tasteless," *New York Times*, January 24, 1999, p. AR38.
8. Quoted in Lacey Rose, "5 Reasons Why Seth MacFarlane Will Be a Great Oscars Host (According to His Sister)," *Hollywood Reporter*, February 20, 2013. www.hollywoodreporter.com.
9. Quoted in Rose, "5 Reasons Why Seth MacFarlane Will Be a Great Oscars Host (According to His Sister)."
10. Quoted in Rose, "5 Reasons Why Seth MacFarlane Will Be a Great Oscars Host (According to His Sister)."
11. Quoted in Jack Coraggio and Kathryn Boughton, "Oscars Host Seth MacFarlane's Path to Fame Began in Tiny Kent, Connecticut," *Litchfield County (CT) Times*, February 21, 2013. www.countytimes.com.
12. Quoted in Coraggio and Boughton, "Oscars Host Seth MacFarlane's Path to Fame Began in Tiny Kent, Connecticut."
13. Quoted in Newman, "Young Talented, Tasteless."
14. Quoted in *Hollywood Reporter*, "Oscars 2013: 25 Things to Know About Host Seth MacFarlane," February 21, 2013. www.hollywoodreporter.com.

15. Quoted in Tannenbaum, "Seth MacFarlane."
16. Quoted in Bill Rodriguez, "Son of Hippies, Still Crazy After 26 Years," *New York Times*, September 3, 2000, p. TE59.
17. Quoted in Bernard Weinraub, "The Young Guy of *Family Guy*: A 30-Year-Old's Cartoon Hit Makes an Unexpected Comeback," *New York Times*, July 7, 2004.
18. Quoted in Newman, "Young, Talented, Tasteless."
19. Quoted in Lacey Rose, "Seth MacFarlane: The Restless Mind of a Complicated Cartoonist," *Hollywood Reporter*, October 12, 2011. www.hollywoodreporter.com.

Chapter Two: *Family Guy*: TV's Most Shocking Show

20. Quoted in Newman, "Young, Talented, Tasteless."
21. Quoted in Hoffman, "No. 1 Offender."
22. Quoted in Hoffman, "No. 1 Offender."
23. Quoted in Josh Dean, "Seth MacFarlane's $2 Billion *Family Guy* Empire," *Fast Company*, November 1, 2008. www.fastcompany .com.
24. Seth MacFarlane, interview by Deborah Solomon, "Questions for Seth MacFarlane: Family Man," *New York Times*, September 13, 2009, p. MM13.
25. Quoted in Hoffman, "No. 1 Offender."
26. Quoted in James Bartlett, "Seth MacFarlane—He's the *Family Guy*," GreatReporter.com, March 12, 2007. http://greatreporter .com.
27. Quoted in Christopher Hooton, "Seth MacFarlane Reveals Why He Killed Brian Griffin in *Family Guy*," *Independent* (London), January 14, 2014. www.independent.co.uk.
28. Quoted in Weinraub, "The Young Guy of *Family Guy*."
29. Quoted in Seth MacFarlane, "How Norman Lear Pushed the Boundaries of Scripted Television," *Vanity Fair*, October 13, 2014. www.vanityfair.com.
30. Quoted in Dean, "Seth MacFarlane's $2 Billion *Family Guy* Empire."
31. Tom Shales, "Tom Shales on TV: *Cleveland Show* Is a Cartoon Blight," *Washington Post*, September 29, 2009. www.washington post.com.

32. Quoted in Tannenbaum, "Seth MacFarlane."

33. Quoted in Hoffman, "No. 1 Offender."

Chapter Three: MacFarlane Steps in Front of the Camera

34. Quoted in David Germain, "Is There Anything Seth MacFarlane Can't Do? Singer, Animator, Talking Teddy Bear: *Family Guy* Boss MacFarlane Expands Resume with *Ted*," Associated Press, in Yahoo! Finance, June 28, 2012. http://finance.yahoo.com.

35. Logan Nicklaus, "*SNL* Recap: Frank Ocean, John Mayer and Seth MacFarlane Kick Off New Season," *Rolling Stone*, September 16, 2012. www.rollingstone.com.

36. Quoted in Camille Mann, "Ryan Lochte Thinks Seth MacFarlane's Impersonation Was 'All Wrong,'" CBS News, September 17, 2012. www.cbsnews.com.

37. Quoted in Mann, "Ryan Lochte Thinks Seth MacFarlane's Impersonation Was 'All Wrong.'"

38. Quoted in Hoffman, "No. 1 Offender."

39. Quoted in Germain, "Is There Anything Seth Macfarlane Can't Do?"

40. Rex Reed, "*Ted* the Triumphant: MacFarlane's Silver Screen Debut Tickles This Critic's Fancy," *New York Observer*, June 26, 2012. http://observer.com.

41. Roger Ebert, "*Ted* Movie Review & Film Summary," Roger Ebert.com, June 27, 2012. www.rogerebert.com.

42. A.O. Scott, "The Lady or the Teddy?," *New York Times*, June 28, 2012. www.movies.nytimes.com.

43. Nicole Sperling, "Why Ted Sounds So Similar to *Family Guy*'s Peter Griffin," *Los Angeles Times*, June 28, 2012. http://articles.latimes.com.

44. Quoted in Anthony Breznican, "The Oscar Guy," *Entertainment Weekly*, February 22, 2013, p. 34.

45. Quoted in Aly Weisman, "Seth MacFarlane's 'We Saw Your Boobs' Song Outraged Women in Hollywood," *Business Insider*, February 28, 2013. www.businessinsider.com.

46. Quoted in Gloria Goodale, "Will Oscar Host Seth MacFarlane Be Asked Back? Probably Not," *Christian Science Monitor*, February 25, 2013, p. 1.

47. Quoted in Ben Child, "Oscars Producers Defend Seth MacFarlane's 'Irreverent' Stint as Host," *Guardian* (London), March 18, 2013. www.theguardian.com.

48. Quoted in Goodale, "Will Oscar Host Seth MacFarlane Be Asked Back? Probably Not."

49. Quoted in *Access Hollywood*, "Seth MacFarlane Defends His Oscar Nominations Hitler Joke," January 11, 2013. www.accesshollywood.com.

50. Quoted in Breznican, "The Oscar Guy."

51. Steven Rea, "Jokes Are First to Die in MacFarlane's *West*," *Philadelphia Inquirer*, May 30, 2014.

52. Rea, "Jokes Are First to Die in MacFarlane's *West*."

53. Rick Bentley, "New DVD Releases Oct. 7: *Million Dollar Arm*, *A Million Ways to Die in the West*, *Edge of Tomorrow*," *Fresno (CA) Bee*, October 1, 2014, www.fresnobee.com.

Chapter Four: Expanding His Fan Base

54. Quoted in Examiner.com, "*Family Guy* Creator Seth MacFarlane—Lashing Out at Arizona Immigration Law," May 3, 2010. www.examiner.com.

55. Quoted in John Benson, "Lalo Alcaraz Takes On Immigration Issues with *Bordertown*," *Huffington Post*, October 2, 2014. www.huffingtonpost.com.

56. Lucas Molandes, "Seth MacFarlane's *Bordertown* Tackles Immigration,"*Tú Vez*, November 2014. www.tuvez.com.

57. Quoted in Benson, "Lalo Alcaraz Takes On Immigration Issues with *Bordertown*."

58. Quoted in *Huffington Post*, "*Bordertown* Animated Series to Tackle America's Cultural Shift, Critics Fear Negative Stereotypes," May 29, 2014. www.huffingtonpost.com.

59. Quoted in Benson, "Lalo Alcaraz Takes On Immigration Issues with *Bordertown*."

60. Quoted in Jeanne Jakle, "*Family Guy* Creator Takes a Run at the Border," *San Antonio Express-News*, November 5, 2014. www.mysanantonio.com.

61. Quoted in Matt Barone, "Interview: Seth MacFarlane Talks *Ted*, Realistic CGI Movie Characters & Keeping *Family Guy* Relevant," *Complex*, June 5, 2012. www.complex.com.

62. Quoted in Ed Pilkington, "Patrick Stewart: 'I Can Store Emotions. No Experience Is Ever Wasted,'" Here Is the City, May 18, 2014. http://hereisthecity.com.

63. David Wiegand, "*Cosmos* Returns—with a Big Bang," *San Francisco Chronicle*, March 7, 2014. www.sfgate.com.

64. Quoted in *Irish Independent* (Dublin), "A Million Ways to Success: How Seth MacFarlane Won Over Hollywood," June 4, 2014, p. 40.

65. Quoted in Lily Rothman, "Neil deGrasse Tyson Looks Back at *Cosmos*," *Time*, June 10, 2014. http://time.com.

66. Quoted in Snierson, "Best Crossover Ever."

67. Quoted in Josh Ferri, "Bringing Future Oscar Host Seth MacFarlane to Broadway 'Would Be a Dream Come True' for Producer Neil Meron," Broadway.com, October 5, 2012. www.broadway.com.

68. Quoted in Todd Aaron Jensen, *On Gratitude: Sheryl Crow, Jeff Bridges, Alicia Keys, Daryl Hall, Ray Bradbury, Anna Kendrick, B.B. King, Elmore Leonard, Deepak Chopra, and 42 More Celebrities Share What They're Most Thankful For*. Avon, MA: Adams Media, 2010, p. 129.

IMPORTANT EVENTS IN THE LIFE OF SETH MACFARLANE

1973
Seth Woodbury MacFarlane is born on October 26 in Kent, Connecticut.

1975
As a toddler, MacFarlane draws Fred Flintstone and Woody Woodpecker on grocery bags.

1982
He is hired to draw the weekly comic strip *Walter Crouton* by the *Kent Good Times Dispatch*, a job he continues until graduating from high school.

1985
His work as a cartoonist is profiled in his hometown newspaper, the *Litchfield County Times*.

1991
MacFarlane enrolls in the Rhode Island School of Design after graduating from Kent School, a private prep school.

1996
MacFarlane is hired as an animator and writer by Hanna-Barbera after graduating from Rhode Island School of Design.

1999
Family Guy debuts after the Super Bowl.

2002
Fox cancels *Family Guy* due to poor ratings but brings it back three years later.

2005
American Dad! premieres.

2009
A *Family Guy* spinoff, *The Cleveland Show*, starts its three-year run.

2011
MacFarlane releases his first CD, *Music Is Better than Words*.

2012
MacFarlane's CGI movie *Ted* is a box office smash, earning $200 million.

2013
MacFarlane stars in the movie *A Million Ways to Die in the West*, which he also wrote and directed.

2014
The *Family Guy–Simpsons* crossover episode is watched by 8.5 million people.

2015
The immigration-themed animated series *Bordertown* debuts on Fox.

FOR FURTHER RESEARCH

Periodicals

Joel Achenbach, "Star Power," *Smithsonian*, March 2014.

Matt Barone, "Interview: Seth MacFarlane Talks *Ted*, Realistic CGI Movie Characters & Keeping *Family Guy* Relevant," *Complex*, June/July 2012.

Michael Cavna, "*Bordertown:* Lalo Alcaraz on Joining Seth MacFarlane's New Fox Immigration Comedy," *Washington Post*, November 14, 2013.

Sandy Cohen, "Seth MacFarlane Juggles 6 Jobs on His Way to the Academy Awards," *Florence (AL) Times Daily*, February 19, 2013.

David Germain, "Is There Anything Seth MacFarlane Can't Do? Singer, Animator, Talking Teddy Bear: *Family Guy* Boss MacFarlane Expands Resume with *Ted*," Associated Press, in Yahoo! Finance, June 28, 2012.

Lesley Goldberg, "Starz Orders Two Seasons of Seth MacFarlane Comedy *Blunt Talk*," *Hollywood Reporter*, April 29, 2014.

Rob Owens, "MacFarlane Cuts a Wide Animation Swath," *Variety*, September 29, 2010.

Michael Schneider, "Exclusive: Fox Gives 13-Episode Order to Animated Series *Bordertown*," *TV Guide*, November 8, 2013.

Dan Snierson, "Best Crossover Ever," *Entertainment Weekly*, September 12, 2014.

Nicole Sperling, "Why Ted Sounds So Similar to *Family Guy*'s Peter Griffin," *Los Angeles Times*, June 28, 2012.

Websites

Cosmos: A Spacetime Odyssey (http://channel.nationalgeographic.com/channel/cosmos-a-spacetime-odyssey). The National Geographic Channel's website for *Cosmos* introduces visitors to host Neil deGrasse Tyson, an astrophysicist who as a teen met Carl Sagan, the original *Cosmos* host. Students can watch a featured episode of the new show, explore the legacy of *Cosmos*, and even create their own virtual universe.

Family Guy (www.fox.com/family-guy). The official Fox website for *Family Guy* features video clips, scheduled showings, complete episodes, interviews with Seth MacFarlane, and links to apps and social media sites. Visitors can also listen to the series' writers discuss their favorite moments in the show and see panel discussions they participated in at Comic Con conventions.

Kent School (www.kent-school.edu). The website maintained by the private preparatory school attended by Seth MacFarlane features a history of the school, which was founded in 1906, and descriptions of the art and drama departments, where MacFarlane honed his early talents. Visitors can also find many photos of students involved in academic life at Kent.

Lalo Alcaraz (http://laloalcaraz.com). The website for Lalo Alcaraz, *Bordertown* writer and creator of the first nationally syndicated, politically themed Hispanic daily comic strip, *La Cucaracha*. Visitors can listen to Alcaraz talk about his life as a cartoonist, view *La Cucaracha* and editorial cartoons Alcaraz has drawn, and send Alcaraz e-mail.

Motion Capture Society (http://www.motioncapturesociety.com). The website for the Motion Capture Society, an international nonprofit group dedicated to the same technology used in the movie *Ted* to record Seth MacFarlane's movements. Students can learn industry terms, see samples of work done by studios that use motion capture in video games and movies, and acquaint themselves with the history of motion capture, which dates back to 1774.

INDEX

PICTURE CREDITS

ABOUT THE AUTHOR

Gail Snyder is a freelance writer and advertising copywriter who has written nearly twenty books for young readers. A lifelong fan of cartoons, she lives in Chalfont, Pennsylvania, with her husband, Hal.